YOU'VE GOT THIS!

Molly Biehl

all the best!
♡ Molly Biehl

You've Got This!

Copyright © 2017 by Molly Biehl

No part of this publication may be reproduced, stored in a retrieval system or transmitted in any form or by any means, electronic, mechanical, photocopying, recording, scanning or otherwise.

All rights reserved, including the right to reproduce this book or portions thereof in any form whatsoever.

Dedication

Z, W, and R – my 3 big "whys"
Mom, Dad, Kim, Amy and Zach – the original Biehls
My friends who are family – you know who you are
Mwale and Chantel – thank you

Table of Contents

Foreword vii

Life Happens 1

Grief is No Joke 11

Devising a Plan 25

Life's Verdict 33

Reality Check 45

Behind the Wheel of Forgiveness 65

The Bad Side of a 'Good Soldier' 75

Forgiving Yourself 89

Epilogue 95

About The Author 101

About The Book 105

Speaking Topics & Workshops 107

Biography 109

Foreword

I've wanted to write a book for a while now, several years in fact. The idea of laying it all out in front of me — drafting some masterpiece, something to boggle the academy and inspire my audience — that's what drew me to writing.

However, when deciding what topic to change the world with, I soon realized one thing: I'm no expert. I can't tell you how to solve the crisis in Syria or make the "human condition" any less mysterious. Yet here I am, with a book and (hopefully) an audience.

So what did I decide to write about? The only thing I can truly call my specialty is my life. A friend once told me that we are each an expert in our own lives; we just have to find our voices. But it's scary to write a book. You're afraid to be judged on multiple levels, from the subject matter, to your attitude toward it, right down to how well you can craft a sentence or express a thought. Regardless of these fears, I'm forging ahead with the hope that my voice will emerge along the way.

> *Through all the heartaches and the tears, through gloomy days and fruitless years; I do give thanks for now I know, these were the things that helped me grow.*
>
> *– David Lockett*

LIFE HAPPENS

There are times when life hands us very bad news. You might be plunging a toilet, reading in bed, or playing with your kids. You might be cleaning the ants out of your sink. You could be a kid on the beach scrawling "I luv u" in the sand. Suddenly, you're told something that changes everything. You hear the news and suddenly you see your whole life-narrative in front of you — past, present, and future — and you know the plot of your story just went from comic to tragic. Forever.

For me, there was a long time when life was disproportionately handing me bad news. I was in my twenties when life began sending handfuls of tragic twists my way. I was twenty-three when the first one landed. At the time the unimaginable happened, I was filling in at a receptionist desk for my friend who had gone to lunch. Expecting to be rerouting phone calls to other people's voicemails, I was surprised when a call was for me.

You know something's gone horribly wrong when the lady on the other end of the line needs to restart her sentence three times to be able to get the words out. Finally, she pushes through: "This is the State Department. We have been trying to reach your parents. We're sorry to have to call you at work, but we didn't want you to hear it through the news. There's been an accident involving your sister."

Then and there I knew she was dead. "There were students," the woman continued. "There was a rally..." she went on, but beyond that I don't remember much, just rushing into the bathroom and vomiting in a stall. My life stood still, stalled by the fact that my body and mind were being squeezed by the unthinkable. It was a pressure that turned me from the inside out.

> *Even the darkest night will end and the sun will rise.*
>
> *– Victor Hugo*

I had to get my dad on the phone. I'd comprehended that much. Eventually someone helped me to a seat with a phone. I don't remember much from our conversation but I do remember telling my dad that Amy was my hero and my dad telling me "she was mine, too."

A couple of days before Amy was killed I had a really bad dream. I woke up convinced something bad had happened to her. It bothered me so much I phoned her apartment in South Africa. Her roommate answered. Realizing how late it was there, I hung up. I didn't want to disturb anybody. That was my last chance to speak to her and I didn't take it. She was murdered by a mob of young men on August 25, 1993. They stoned her car, stoned her, and then stabbed her to death. The regret of not speaking to her that night haunts me to this day.

But so what? So life had handed me some bad news. Why does that make my story notable? Bad news is a part of everyone's life. Just be lucky that you're not the subject, right?

But often we discredit our own bad news. We choose not to share with people around us because we think our stories don't stand as tall as the next guy's. We walk around suffering in silence for fear of being a burden.

Why not consider that, though we might be alone in our particular circumstances, we are not alone in our suffering and our desire to get through it? And further, that perhaps by sharing something about our journey, someone else might get to understand something about theirs? Perhaps in the midst of dealing with the unimaginable, we can find comfort in numbers and examples of hope. We can even be a source of hope ourselves. This is why I am sharing my story.

In the years following Amy's death, more bad news came, and it kept coming. I had a miscarriage, my father passed away, Hurricane

Katrina hit our family home in the New Orleans suburbs, and my marriage of fifteen years came to an end. Just when one traumatic event was subsiding, another was exploding. It seemed like life had flipped a switch; I found myself in constant survival mode, bracing myself, preparing to react to the next tragic plot-point. Each terrible thing felt exactly like the last, so I began looking outside of myself for answers, which in hindsight meant keeping myself on the move.

After Amy was killed, I left life as a young professional in Washington, DC, and moved to New Orleans to start grad school, but also to escape the memories of Amy having lived there too. A couple years later, on a happier occasion, I moved back to my home state of California to get married and start a family. After the birth of our second child, my dad died, and soon after his death we moved our family back to New Orleans. It seemed like the outward change of setting and lifestyle would make me feel better inside. Two years later, Hurricane Katrina hit and our way of life was displaced. I was back to square one and moving back to California.

It wasn't all bad during this time. I earned my master's degree in sociology and ran marathons. I birthed three healthy children. A number of my loved ones got married. I gained a few nieces and nephews. Still, even with the positives, the sheer volume of negativity life had thrust upon me made me feel like I was destined for a life without control, a life where my main objective was to manage the unexpected tragedies that kept piling up. I would have to maintain a sense of normalcy for my family. I was to minimize the disruption, the pain, the emotional damage in myself and the people around me. I'd accepted it, but at the pace my life was going, I didn't think I would be able to accomplish much else. I'd moved a lot but gotten nowhere, and as each event happened my response was the same. Keep your chin up, support your family, set an example for your kids, and bounce back. It was like I was one of those old Weeble toys.

I had grown up playing with those. Maybe you remember them, little plastic dolls with rounded bottoms. You could push them every which direction and they'd just keep popping back up. The commercials would say, "Weebles wobble, but they don't fall down." And that's how I felt: constantly teetering, but when on the cusp of collapse, I'd always spring back up. Today, I'm proud of this. It meant I was resilient. It's one of the first adjectives I'd use to describe myself and one of the best things that life gave to me. When your resilience is tested as many times as mine, you come to the comforting realization that you can depend upon it. You know you can get through the next thing.

But resilience doesn't give us the whole answer. It's the coping tool we turn to when the other shoe drops, yet resilience only lets you find your way back to "normal." It ensures you'll survive, but you stop short of thriving. It seemed there ought to be something more, that there must be a different way of processing grief. No one wants to be weebling back and forth in the same spot their whole life. They want to be able to move forward with some sense of autonomy, to stop oscillating between grief and anxiety over the next thing to grieve. They want to pursue happiness and fulfillment even after tragedy. That fulfillment, I've discovered, takes a deeper journey.

And that is the journey I'd like to share with you.

GRIEF IS NO JOKE

Now it might seem a little heavy to start with a discussion of grief. Why start with the heavy parts? Well, because that's how grief hits you. It hits you hard, fast, and without warning, leaving you to slowly work your way through it.

Bear with me as we do just that.

So what is grief? It comes in many forms. It can follow losing a loved one or a home, getting a divorce, or even your candidate losing the big election. Grief can be overwhelming. It keeps you from concentrating on a task at hand. Sometimes it keeps you down. Other times it might have you aimlessly running around, wondering what you can do next to fill your time and avoid the pain of being still. Imagine the world order as you know it shifting. Imagine the center to your universe dropping out, and imagine clamoring around to find something to hold onto, but there is nothing except a big, black void. That, readers, is grief.

When you're grieving, you forget you ever had any answers. You wonder how you're going to get out of bed, what to tell your kids, or how to raise your kids while feeling like this. You wonder why this happened to the person you love, and why it happened to you. You'll look at the sky and plead for help, for something or someone to take the pain away or make things right again. You'll crawl into bed and exhaust yourself through the tears that settle in. And just as soon as you think you've gained some composure, a song on the radio, a photograph, or meeting someone with your loved one's name sets you back to square one. You'll start to judge the living against the dead. You'll judge someone for wasting precious time, for saying something insensitive, for taking someone for granted, thinking it's all so unfair when all you wish for is to hug the one you lost and tell them how much you love them. And when

> *I've learned that no matter how badly your heart is broken, the world doesn't stop for your grief.*
>
> –Paulo Coelho

you're really at your lowest, you'll start judging yourself. That, friends, is grief.

Then there are the "what-ifs." What if you'd convinced them not to go there, or to eat healthier? What if you'd made that phone call to let them know you were worried about them? Then maybe the course of events would have changed, and maybe on that day they would have done something different and would still be here to poke fun at the fact that you're such a worry wart. Or the worst one, you wonder: What if it could have been me? They had so much going for them, so much to look forward to. Why couldn't it have been me? That, people, is grief.

Then there's everyone else, how the world treats you and the brutal fact that it keeps on going when you're desperate for everything to stop. When you are out in your neighborhood it feels like you're wearing a sign on your chest that says "Fragile! Please tiptoe around me."

People don't just look at you differently — they walk around you differently, smile at you differently, talk to you differently, or don't even talk to you at all. Your story might seem like a burden to people or even a source of gossip. You'll get in a work elevator after your loved one has died. It'll be your first day back on the job. It'll be the place where you used to be the one to say "Hey guys! What's up?" But now, it's just another place where you have to stand, none of you knowing what to say. There will be a long pause, some eyes shifting uncomfortably, and the inner realization of "Shit. This is my life now."

Then there's the numbness. Your priorities shift. The little things lose importance. You can't remember if you paid your bills, if you ate anything that day, or if you asked your kids about their homework. You get agitated wondering why people get so worked up about seemingly petty things when those very things were once important to you. Information passes you by fifty times before you comprehend any of it. You find yourself going through the motions on special occasions. You want to be excited about your kid's birthday or Christmas dinner, but you are just numb. You haven't felt excitement in days, weeks, or months. You haven't felt much of anything since "it" happened. That, mourners, is grief.

But then something miraculous happens. Your emotions recalibrate, and you begin to reassess. The numbness wears off and you come out of your fog. Eventually, all those longings to have your loved one back, all that time spent wishing you could hold them again, will shift into a greater appreciation for those you have left. Slowly, things will begin to matter again, sometimes even more than they did before. Life's highs are indescribably beautiful, and you let yourself take time to really feel them. It will matter that everyone you love is accounted for. You can touch them, and you actually hear them when they tell you about their day. You begin to laugh at their jokes and even allow yourself to get annoyed when they leave their dirty dishes on the table. Telling them you love them will matter because, unlike those lost to you, your loved ones can hear you, and you don't ever want there to be a minute when they don't know where they stand with you. When in doubt, remember: This is also part of grief.

In grief, saying goodbye to those you care about takes on a different magnitude of importance. You might experience a finality to the words.

I remember being in the airport after my sister's

funeral. I was living in Washington, DC, and had flown to California in the hours following her death. I had been home for a couple of weeks and it was finally time to return to my job and my life. I was standing with my parents waiting for my flight, when it hit me: They never waited with me for a flight before. I'd travelled all over the world by myself, so I hadn't needed them to. But there we were, all standing awkwardly, waiting for the plane to board. Through the silent discomfort, I could sense how fragile the moment was. I hugged them, and tried to force a smile. But at that moment, I realized that the discomfort came from the new awareness that there was no

"Vulnerability sounds like truth and feels like courage. Truth and courage aren't always comfortable, but they're never weakness."

– Brene Brown

guarantee we would see each other again. It was sad, but it showed me how grief makes you vulnerable.

And, if you gain nothing else from reading my story, remember this: Grief isn't just your world turning upside down. It's not just regret, numbness, or social stigma. It can take these forms, but at the end of the day, grief is your displaced love for someone taking you over for a while. In that sense and through hindsight, I think grief can be beautiful.

It's a given that when we grieve for a loved one, we're forced to deal with their physical absence. You're likely to expect this absence once the initial shock wears off. There will always be an extra chair at the dinner table. The phone won't ring when it's supposed to. There is no one to send that birthday card to and one fewer person to appreciate your funny stories. It comes in waves. It never really stops coming, but at least you're aware that it's going to be there. That's not the part of grief I'm going to deal with here.

There's other stuff that accompanies grief that you can't see coming. It's the unforeseen consequences and they're different for everybody. The breakdown of families, secrets coming out, hurt feelings, and the preoccupation with thoughts that you never had before.

Never were unforeseen consequences so evident as when my marriage ended in 2013. My sister was gone, my dad was gone, my grandparents were gone. But for a while, I at least had someone to be close with, someone who kept the "absence of Biehls" from seeming like the "absence of everybody." There was someone who had been there through everything with me, all the way back to my college years when my world felt intact and my support system infinite. But when my husband left, so did comfort and almost everything I recognized as normal.

It was the daily interactions that drove home for me how we can never project grief's impact. We have three kids together, so there will always be a connection between my ex-husband and me. But when he started coming by the house we once shared to be with the kids, it was like I was never married to him. We had drawn boundaries to get past the conflict and the pain. Obviously, we had to. And, while I could always cherish the memories we shared as a family, the closeness I'd felt with him simply vanished. It was like he had died, too.

I felt like an island. I could hang out with friends or talk with my family when I needed some support, but at some point you have to go back to your house, feed the dog, sign the school permission slips and put the kids to bed. And after that's done, it's quiet. It's just you, your king-size bed, and your new normal, a normal clouded by fearful thoughts and shattered dreams.

With my divorce, grief had ushered in what seemed to be insurmountable circumstances. Those moments were the lowest for me. Fortunately, it is when we are at our lowest that we are quickest to bounce back and the Weeble in me set to work.

I knew my marriage was over and my kids wouldn't need me forever. Everyone around me was carrying on with their lives. I also understood I was getting nowhere by going through the exact same process every time something unwelcome happened in my life.

I knew I wanted to somehow get beyond this survival mode, scrambling through my days as a newly single mom with tons on my plate to find myself exhausted in my bed every night, ruminating about my situation.

Lying around staring at the walls wasn't helping me, and it didn't feel like I was going to get very far being passive. So one night I declared to myself that I would work to develop a system for finding peace and maybe — just maybe — happiness again. I was a capable, disciplined woman. Though I didn't want an instructional guide to happiness, as a sociologist, I began I wonder if somewhere there existed any scientifically-based strategies I could implement that would help move me toward my goal. Imagine if my life was no longer defined by how well I managed my pain but by how well I lived and how much happiness I brought to each day! I could not envision what my life would look like beyond grief or how I could possibly get there. Regardless, I knew I owed it to myself to try.

DEVISING A PLAN

The first step in developing a strategy for thriving was figuring out where to start. If I started my process in the dirt, this idea was the seed that would bloom into the rest of my life. It is the idea that when life gets crazy, disappointing, or terrifying, the best way to navigate out of the dirt is with intent.

It's important to remember that intent is not simply about coping or being resilient. It might start there, but after a certain point, it stops being a good thing to stay idle in grief. Sometimes we are told that time heals, that if we are patient the pain subsides and we'll be back on our way. With intent, however, you decide that you have a say in how long you stay there. You have a say in how things go. If you want to feel sad and sorry for yourself, that is fine in that moment. In fact, you must not feel guilty about that. You might find yourself feeling badly for grieving so deeply or for so long when your problems

> *Character cannot be developed in ease and quiet. Only through experience of trial and suffering can the soul be strengthened, vision cleared, ambition inspired, and success achieved.*
>
> *– Helen Keller*

don't seem to compare with those of others in this world. But that is a mistake. Guilt and intent are not compatible. Intent starts with an understanding and acceptance of how you feel, regardless of how you feel. Intent is a decision about where you'd like to be. It is a reminder that you have a purpose outside of your negative experience.

My intent was to have a better understanding of myself so I could return to a vibrant me. I didn't want to provide my kids with a blank-faced example of grief and coping. I wanted to show them that pain is inevitable in life, but it shouldn't ever define one's life. I wanted to live my life as I wanted to, standing *on* my story of coping and resilience — not *in* it.

So I committed to taking a thorough look at the lessons I had learned through all of my loss and the current realities of my life that were difficult to face. I had become accustomed to swallowing hard truths. It was time to be honest with myself.

But it was also time to be fair. I knew that beating myself up for allowing myself to get to this place was not going to get me anywhere, and I also knew that it wasn't going to help to blame anyone else. Although it would feel momentarily better to complain and elicit sympathy from my friends, circumstances were circumstances and I'd still end up home alone at night staring at the walls. So I asked myself what I felt I had done well in dealing with my circumstances to date, things I felt I could be proud of. I would figure out where I started, where I'd been, and how I wanted to define myself in this unfamiliar territory of being on my own.

The more I thought about it, the clearer it became: I needed to start with the exploration of the process of forgiveness. I'd forgiven in the past, and in a situation that many saw as unforgivable. I knew it had been a liberating experience and I'd felt relief, inner peace, and literal amazement at the unforeseen goodness that had come from forgiving my sister's killers. I felt I had done well by myself in doing that, and I thought that could provide me some clues for my future. The challenge was I just wasn't sure how I had gotten there before.

> *You never know how strong you are until being strong is the only choice you have.*
>
> *– Bob Marley*

To add to this challenge, I wasn't feeling particularly generous with my ex-husband. I was firmly planted in my victimhood and didn't really want to forgive him for what I saw as a unilateral decision to end our marriage. I was feeling impatient in my grief this time around and frustrated that I had to go through this one alone, especially because the divorce was not what I had wanted.

There was no doubt about it, the process was going to be difficult. But the mere possibility of freedom from the pain I was experiencing and a life in which I could choose who I wanted to become had already taken hold in my heart. I was thus committed to do the hard work needed to forgive for perhaps the most difficult obstacle I had faced yet by learning from my past.

Before I can talk about forgiveness, we have to discuss injustice. Some people would say that my sister's death was a particularly unjust one, and they'd have several different reasons to say it. One might argue that her death was unfair because it was sudden, because she was young, because it was caused by ignorance, or because it was so brutal. I'd argue that when you love someone, any cause of death can seem unjust, whether it was a long battle with cancer, a sudden heart attack, a car accident, or a terrorist attack. When you're the one grieving it rarely seems fair. But being stuck in the injustice of it all doesn't get you very far. As hard as it is to admit, I think most of us know, that accepting your circumstances will get you farther.

LIFE'S VERDICT

My sister was killed by a mob of young black men in Gugulethu township in Cape Town, South Africa. She was killed because she was white.

To them, she represented the oppressor in the final months of South Africa's apartheid. What they didn't know was that my sister was on their side. They didn't know that she had spent years working to bring about free and fair elections to emerging democracies throughout the African continent, that she wrote briefing papers for the man who would ultimately become South Africa's next prime minister of justice, or that she knew their native language and danced their traditional dances.

After a yearlong criminal trial which began in the months following Amy's death, four men were sentenced to 18 years in prison. Four years into their prison term the men came before South Africa's Truth and Reconciliation Commission, chaired by Desmond Tutu. The commission had the authority to grant amnesty to those whose crimes were deemed politically motivated during the time of apartheid. If they met certain criteria, amnesty applicants could be released from prison and begin their lives anew. My sister was intimately familiar with the Truth and Reconciliation Commission. In fact, she was a vocal supporter of it. To her, it would make possible the honest dialogue needed to help deliver South Africa from its painful past.

In the summer of 1997, Amy's killers came before that commission and the hearing was broadcast around the world. My parents spoke before the panel and before those convicted of killing Amy. They talked about who Amy was as a person, while the men talked about what they did to her and why they did it. It was a short but emotional hearing. After a day and a half of testimony, my dad offered these closing remarks:

"We have the highest respect for your Truth and Reconciliation Commission

and process. We recognize that if this process had not been a pre-negotiated condition, your democratic free elections could not possibly have occurred. Therefore, and believing as Amy did in the absolute importance of those democratic elections occurring, we unabashedly support the process which we recognize to be unprecedented in contemporary human history. At the same time we say to you it's your process, not ours. We cannot, therefore, oppose amnesty if it is granted on merit. In the truest sense, it is for the community of South Africa to forgive its own and this has its basis in traditions of ubuntu and other principles of human dignity. Amnesty is not clearly for Linda and Peter Biehl to grant."

"You face a challenging and extraordinarily difficult decision. How

do you value a human life? What value do you place on Amy and her legacy in South Africa? How do you exercise responsibility to the community in granting forgiveness, in the granting of amnesty? How are we preparing prisoners, such as these young men before us, to re-enter the community as a benefit to the community, acknowledging that the vast majority of South Africa's prisoners are under thirty years of age? Acknowledging as we do that there's massive unemployment in the marginalized community; acknowledging that the recidivism rate is roughly ninety-five percent? So, how do we, as friends, link arms and do something?"

As my parents were leaving to go back to their Cape Town apartment, they passed by the men. One of them handed my dad a wooden ship he had built while in prison, and a couple of them extended their hands to him. My dad shook their hands in return. A year later, the men were granted amnesty and were released from prison. They were able to return to their communities to start their lives anew.

I think each member of my family was prepared for the likelihood that they would be granted amnesty. Still, when it happened, the reality was a painful one to process. My reaction when my dad called me to share the news was a not-so-profound "Oh shit! Are you serious?" I was forced to process this unfathomable news

> *When you forgive, you do not change the past, but you sure do change the future.*
>
> *– Bernard Meltxer*

in the public's eye, while inside I was reeling with shock.

Aside from feeling the immense void that was her absence that day, it felt terribly unfair for the men to be given their lives back — when Amy wasn't.

So much could go wrong going forward. Honoring Amy's legacy as best we knew how was what had kept our family moving forward in the years between the criminal trial and the amnesty hearing. But now we could neither predict nor control what these young men would do and what that would mean for her legacy, for South Africa, and for our family. I remember praying simply that her death be not in vain.

As it turns out, the decision to grant amnesty was a personal gift of immeasurable value, not simply because Amy agreed with its premise and because it felt morally sound, but because their freedom presented me my own trial in dealing with grief. It tested my ability to forgive.

At first there was nothing imminent to challenge my capacity for forgiveness. I would likely not cross paths with Amy's killers given that we lived on separate continents. Perhaps I could arrange to meet them one day, but that wasn't really on my radar. But something soon happened that would change all of that. Not long after their release, the men who took my sister from us wanted to meet with my parents in Gugulethu.

They *took my sister*. It's a euphemism, really. It doesn't accurately describe what they did to her. They could have taken her on a trip to Disneyland. Or on safari. I used to hate saying it like that. They didn't "take" her so much as they murdered Amy in cold blood. Of course it's easy to dwell on a tragedy; it's much harder to accept the consequence. When they killed her, that was tragic. But what was more tragic was that she was gone. Accepting that fact was the goal. So yes, they murdered her, but more relevantly, they took Amy from me, my family and from the many others who loved her.

I'm guessing it was a combination of the stories Amy had told my parents about the injustices of apartheid against South Africa's black youth, her passion for human rights, and the dialogue started through the Truth and Reconciliation Commission hearings that had begun to humanize Amy's killers to my parents and inspired them to accept the initial invitation to meet the men on their turf. My mom couldn't go to this meeting; I had just given birth to their first grandchild in California.

When tragedy strikes, a common question is "What good could possibly come from this?" Given the unfolding of the coming events, I can say in this instance — a lot! As it turned out, the purpose for the meeting was not for the men to extend an apology. Instead, it was to ask my parents for help. The men had learned that, while they were in prison, my parents had begun operating violence prevention and economic empowerment programs in Gugulethu township where they lived and where Amy had died. Through the work of the Amy Biehl Foundation Trust, young people were participating in music, sports, gardening and greening programs, literacy programs, and micro-business opportunities, including producing beautiful bags, pillows, and jewelry for sale. The community's needs were identified by its members through focus groups and dialogue. The efforts were fledgling but the impact, significant.

LIFE'S VERDICT

After serving their prison time, the men, former leaders in their youth movement, had returned to Gugulethu and were no longer being looked to by their peers for guidance in boycotting school and making bombs in the struggle against the white oppressor. Now, they were being looked to for help in finding jobs and creating constructive things to do because though South Africa had become a free, democratic society, resources and opportunities for people living in the township remained scarce. After an explanation of their situation and an exchange of ideas, my dad left that meeting agreeing to partner with them. His eloquent remarks at the Truth and Reconciliation Commission were now an awkward reality. They would "link arms" and move forward together. On one continent, a baby was born, on another, a new relationship.

REALITY CHECK

I do not know if the men apologized to my dad that day or to either of my parents ever. I know they have not apologized to me. But somehow their reaching out, the example my parents set, and my desire to honor Amy by understanding the context in which she was killed all combined to make me curious about pressing forward through this test to forgive.

No one, my parents included, ever expected me (or my siblings) to forgive, and certainly not so soon. In fact, many people would tell me I was "dancing on my sister's grave" for even considering letting her killers off the hook. Also, in the months after their meeting, I was harboring resentment toward the men involved in the attack and, admittedly, even my parents for spending time working alongside them when I wanted them around to witness their grandchild's milestones or just to spend normal family time together. Now a parent myself, I completely understand the importance and the challenge in making the choice they did. But at the time I wondered how it could be that these men could take

> *Promise me you'll always remember: You're braver than you believe, and stronger than you seem, and smarter than you think.*
>
> *– A.A. Milne*

Amy away from me and then take my parents' attention, too. They spent time having dinner together and even going to the theater. The men eventually had children of their own who call my mother *Makhulu*, a Xhosa name for wise mother. It's the same name my own children call her.

Resentment and all, I still couldn't help but feel a pull to rise above the circumstances and see what this forgiveness thing was about. I would like to be clear, I wasn't trying to be brave. This was about me listening to my gut and moving through what had the potential to otherwise become paralysis. I continued to hear the words told to us in 1993 by Lympho Hani, widow of South African Communist Party leader and major youth galvanizer Chris Hani, who was assassinated in his driveway in front of his daughter just months prior to Amy's death. *When you are bitter, you can't think straight.*

You can't be constructive. In retrospect, while I wanted to honor Amy and follow my parents' example, it was likely more about forgiving these men to escape the incessant what-ifs, the could-have-beens, the comparisons, the jealousy, the bitterness, and the fear of losing my parents, too.

So, with the intent to forgive and alleviate the resentment, I did the only thing I could think to do at the time: I simply began to tell myself I forgave. People say we become our thoughts and the things we say to ourselves, and just saying the words did over time provide me a small sense of relief. But how would I know if the forgiveness was real? Was just deciding you wanted it and saying it enough? It would be years later that I could confirm that forgiveness is more than just words. Forgiveness is a feeling.

REALITY CHECK

In April of 2014, and not long after my divorce, I had the opportunity to speak directly with one of the men responsible for Amy's death. He was going to be at UC Berkeley at an event celebrating the legacy of Nelson Mandela through highlighting the hard work of reconciliation. He and my mom were featured speakers, as they often are together at events around the world. I had told my mom I wanted to attend this event as part of my quest to face things in my past which I felt could help me in the present. She never expected my siblings or me to attend, but I think she was happy to have the company.

I was beyond anxious about what was ahead of me. I knew I faced the possibility of doing myself a complete disservice by derailing any emotional progress I had made to date. I went on long walks preparing myself for what it would be like to look him in the eye. I practiced different greetings I could extend. I pictured myself asking him the long list of questions I had pondered (and actually had kept in written form) for two decades, including some big ones: What goes through your mind when you are inflicting physical harm on a person? What did you do when she was moaning in pain and pleading for help while you were throwing stones? Did you just stare at her? Did you smile? I wondered if I would possibly have the desire to extend my hand to him.

I fantasized about having this intense conversation that would end in apology and an expression of remorse, and then I would present him with the still-bloodied bracelets she was wearing the day she was killed. The thoughts went on and on. I finally decided that I would bring a friend as backup and convinced myself that I would simply "show up." No script, no expectations. Just be present and let the moment unfold.

As it turned out, the greeting was perfect. I had told my mom I would prefer to meet with him privately prior to the actual event. Perhaps coffee or a cocktail? We agreed a glass of wine would be best. So I arrived, two bottles of wine in hand, and my mom knocked on his hotel door, which was just across from hers. "Hi. I'm Molly," I said when he opened the door, my hands too full of wine to offer a handshake or do much of anything. "Molly!" he said with a giant grin.

We sat in the hotel lobby and after some smalltalk facilitated by my mom, he got to telling me stories about my dad. By this meeting, it had been a number of years since my dad had died of cancer, and it was clear he missed him dearly, too. He told me how afraid he'd been to meet with my father that day in Gugulethu years before. I asked him why, my mind filling in his answers beforehand: "How do I look him in the eye? What can I say to him? How do you apologize for something like this?"

And, as I'd grown accustomed to this journey by now, I was in for another surprise. His initial fear, it turns out, was that my father might have shown up carrying a gun in search of revenge. For a second I almost laughed, knowing my father's nature. But I quickly came to realize how relevant this man's fear was. Of course he was afraid of that; he lived with that fear every day of his life. It's why militias are formed, why people kill for ideas, why men die so their sons might live. It was survival, plain and simple. Pure, reactionary survival.

It was the reason these men had killed my sister.

I had always known her murder was a mistake, but I hadn't fully understood why the mistake had to happen. It was at that moment that I realized the full fear. I had been told and read about it, but now I was physically experiencing that Amy's death wasn't just a tragic mistake, but a cruel casualty of an incessant struggle. It was in meeting him that I experienced his vulnerability and I saw our shared humanity. We were both afraid, we both loved our families, we both loved my parents, and we both wanted to live our futures free of grief.

I felt fifty pounds lighter that night as we talked in the hotel lobby and throughout the event. I watched as he and my mom spoke at the front of the room full of academics, activists, strangers, and friends. As they spoke, a picture of my dad was projected on the screen behind them. It was surreal and comforting at once. We spent the rest of the evening seated next to each other at a table surrounded by perfect strangers. We shared stories and we laughed. I left the event almost giddy, and, perhaps most importantly, not feeling an ounce of guilt for feeling happy in such a strange circumstance. It was that night that the scary dreams, the painful images and countless questions that I had carried with me for two decades simply vanished. None of it has ever returned. He had been free from his prison for years now and I was finally free from mine, too.

Forgiveness, I could confirm, meant feeling light and feeling free. It was a deeper level of knowing and accepting your situation. It reminded me of that satisfied feeling when you hug your kids goodbye and send them off to school knowing you've done your job; they are ready to face the world and now it's up to them. Forgiveness is peace and contentment.

REALITY CHECK

So there you have it: first my parents' forgiveness, and eventually my own. A partnership and ultimately a friendship was formed, one that's remained intact to this day and now includes my teenage children. At first, forgiveness seemed just a byproduct of the journey. But when I set out to explore how it happened, I realized what a necessary step it was for me. If nothing else, I am proud to say two things about myself today: First, I had the resilience to stand tall in my grief. Second, I learned what it felt like to forgive.

The big bummer is, just because you come to terms with and forgive one person or situation in your life, that doesn't mean everything else magically straightens itself out. But like crossing the finish line after running a marathon, even while you are limping and delirious and cursing yourself for putting yourself through hell, you're ready to sign up for your next one. You've caught the bug.

In my continued quest for understanding and how to reclaim my vibrant self, I had been reading a lot of positive psychology and had signed up for an online course called the "Science of Happiness" offered through EdX by the UC Berkeley Greater Good Science Center. One of the supplemental readings was Sonja Lyubomirsky's *The How of Happiness,* a book on science-backed strategies to achieve happiness. (So, such strategies do actually exist!) I found it all quite relevant and useful to my experiences, but when I got to a section called "Happiness Activity #7, Learning to Forgive," I came upon the following:

> *"When I was a doctoral student at Stanford a twenty-six-year-old woman,*

Amy Biehl, who had graduated with a BA in international relations and had a taken a Fulbright scholarship to research women's rights and fight segregation in South Africa, was pulled from her car and stabbed to death by a mob in Gugulethu township, near Cape Town."

Holy crap! Here I was trying to learn about forgiveness, when the class was looking to my family's story as an example. It was a strangely exciting feeling. I asked myself, "Okay, what is the scientific basis for our story becoming an example to others? How is she going to describe our process of forgiveness when I don't even understand it?!" If overcoming one of my life's greatest obstacles was literally a textbook example of forgiveness, then perhaps I could repeat it in other areas in my life. With this newfound hope, I continued reading:

> *"...when you are wronged....it appears the first inclination in human beings is to respond negatively to such injuries, to reciprocate with an equal harm. The two other typical responses are a desire to avoid the person or to seek revenge."*

I had the avoidance thing down following my divorce for sure.

> *"It would seem obvious that such responses breed negative consequences. Trying to distance yourself from the transgressor and especially trying to retaliate — ultimately makes you unhappy. It can damage or destroy relationships and it may even harm society at large..."*

> *"Forgiveness may be the one factor that can disrupt the cycles of avoidance and vengeance in which*

we often find ourselves...forgiveness involves suppressing or mitigating one's motivations for avoidance and revenge...and, ideally, replacing them with more positive or benevolent attitudes, feelings, and behaviors."

After describing what forgiveness was, Dr. Lyubomirsky articulated what forgiveness was *not*. It is not, she stated, reconciliation. You do not have to establish or reestablish a relationship with the transgressor. She explained that forgiveness does not involve a pardon or indicate condoning. There would be no need for forgiveness if that were the case. Forgiveness does not mean excusing or denying what happened. And to say "forgive and forget" is certainly not synonymous with forgiveness as it suggests the memory will lessen when for many of us it will not. "Truly forgiving someone," she said, "involves contemplating the injury at some length while forgetting the injury would make that process rather difficult."

She then asked, "How, then, do you know if you've forgiven someone? *It's when you have experienced a shift in thinking*, such that your desire to harm that person has decreased and your desire to do him good (or to benefit your relationship) has increased."

> *The weak can never forgive. Forgiveness is an attribute of the strong.*
>
> – Mahatma Gandhi

Dr. Lyubomirsky went on to say that empirical research confirms what Mrs. Hani had told my family in South Africa back in 1993. Being bitter hurts *you* more than the other person. If you choose to forgive, it is *scientifically* less likely you will be anxious and angry and more likely you will be happier and healthier.

Well hallelujah! There it was, spelled out right in front of me. I immediately shared it with my mom telling her we aren't crazy... the benefits are real and proven! I then emailed Dr. Lyubomirsky to thank her for putting into words so specifically what I didn't fully understand and what I couldn't explain myself. I had now come across a rational and science-based explanation for what I knew intuitively to be a response that was good for me in trying to move forward. She'd made me want to shout in the faces of everyone who called us crazy for forgiving Amy's killers and say, "Look! Forgiveness is good for you, people! And, by the way, it is good for society, too!"

You are not compromising anything by granting forgiveness. You are gaining peace of mind. You are not justifying or minimizing, nor do you have to forget about what happened. It doesn't mean you love the person you lost any less. I say, *it just means you are choosing to love yourself a little more.* You don't ever have to reconcile with the other person to forgive (though in our case, we have). You just need to work toward a "shift in thinking."

And that's what really gave me hope. I had experienced a literal and almost instantaneous shift in thinking after meeting the man at UC Berkeley. Fear and dismay had become contentment and pride, and my desire to do good by him had most definitely increased. In fact, I was actually looking forward to seeing him again. That was my signal to know I could put the grief surrounding my sister's death to bed. You see, one thing about the path out of grief is that there's so much uncertainty. Even when your path starts to seem easier to tread,

REALITY CHECK

you might start questioning whether you're on the right trail or heading toward a dead end. Nope. In this case I was certain I'd come through the other side of grief.

BEHIND THE WHEEL OF FORGIVENESS

What Dr. Lyubomirsky gave me was a sense that my mind was naturally working toward ends that would benefit it. In other words, she made me trust my instincts. I'd shifted my thoughts many a time since Amy's death, but now I could finally trust myself and my capacity to forgive. Forgiveness is rational and not self-compromising, and I needed to stop being afraid that I was hurting myself by forgiving others. And now I had another shift of thought: a shift toward autonomy and control. Now I was behind the wheel of my grief. I had tools with which to navigate if not expedite the process. I could move through grief with a goal to forgive, and with intention I could get there faster. I could now shift out of neutral and into gear to handle my grief around the breakdown of my marriage. It was exciting; this was going to work!

Or was it? You can decide to forgive, you can want to forgive, but what do you actually DO to forgive? Not every situation is going to find you face-to-face with your sister's killer or with someone pleading for your forgiveness, and all you have to say is yes or no. It's not every time that you will see the shared humanity in an exchange that will make saying "I forgive you" feel somewhat natural.

Sonja Lyubomirsky book had suggested several exercises on how to forgive. They are, indeed, helpful and doable, but I found that when I didn't have the book with me I couldn't always capture the generosity of spirit required to do the activities or even remember what they were. And, since I'm often on the go, it became difficult to stop and re-read the instructions.

I needed something handy to help me make forgiveness a daily thing. I wanted it to become a habit. I wanted something that would guide me step-by-step through the process and I wanted it to be foolproof. It's funny how when you are on a quest for discovery and moving in the right direction, synchronicities happen. For me on my quest, it was often a click on my computer and I was exactly where I needed to be, reading something that seemed to be written just for me. This is how I came across Vishen Lakhiani. Lakhiani is a world-renowned speaker, author and the founder of Mindvalley Academy, an education and technology company that publishes books on spiritual development, life lessons and personal journeys. One of the topics Lakhiani himself discusses is — you guessed it — forgiveness.

I joke with my kids that Vishen is my best friend, he just doesn't know it. It is his guided forgiveness exercise that has made forgiveness a daily habit for me. I now consciously forgive something or someone every single morning and, trust me, I've never run out of material. It takes just a few minutes and starts my day off in a space of generosity and gratitude. It makes me feel empowered and an active contributor to the way I experience challenges in my life.

Vishen's exercise is a guided visualization in which you start by closing your eyes and conjuring up an image of the person you wish to forgive. You visualize yourself telling that person, "I forgive you, and I ask that you forgive me." As you imagine saying this, you try to see your forgiveness moving toward them while feeling the release of your pent up anger, your frustration, and your grief. Next, you visualize the person you are forgiving saying the same thing *back* to you: "I forgive you and I ask that you forgive me."

> *There is no sense in punishing your future for the mistakes of your past. Forgive yourself, grow from it, and then let it go.*
>
> *– Melanie Koulouris*

You see yourself taking that in and again try to experience all negativity leaving your body.

Now it might seem a little corny, and perhaps it really is. But I've come to be fine with corny so long as it works. And while the exercise in its structure is simple, it is not that simple to do, especially at the start. In fact, it's why he recommends practicing with really small things that you'd likely soon forget about anyway, like someone cutting you off on the freeway or your kid not taking out the garbage. It might not be effective if you just dive into it by trying to forgive, say, abuse by a parent.

In the beginning, visualizing was difficult for me. I could not "see" much of anything with my eyes closed. Who could? And while I still don't always see an image of the person I'm forgiving, I can at least sense what it's like being around them. At first, I had also taken major issue with the fact that this exercise required me to ask the other person for *their* forgiveness. What?! Why would they need to forgive me? I was not the transgressor! But if you stick with it and trust the process, you start to get it.

This exercise is always about you benefitting, not the other person. It's not about doing the person any favors, though I'll clue you in that you do, and by the time you notice it you'll be okay with it. And though it's not the intent, when you are in a relaxed and forgiving space — when your guard is down - you might see a side of a situation that you had never seen before.

> *It's one of the greatest gifts you can give to yourself. Forgive everybody.*
>
> *– Maya Angelou*

I had nothing to lose and everything to gain when I started doing this exercise, so I just pretended and imagined away, day after day, until what originally felt like fist-tightening frustration bordering on implosion ultimately shrunk to a slight aggravation that would just melt away in minutes. I could actually conjure the feeling that I'd forgiven and experience that shift in thought that I had experienced before. At last, I could feel forgiveness for the man who used to be my husband and I could, at times, even sense why I had once loved him so dearly.

Even if you never get that far, doing this exercise or one similar will make you damn certain that forgiveness isn't a hack premise upon which to obtain peace of mind and greater control of your emotions. Just getting to a space where you let go of even a little anger will feel uncomfortable at first. For some reason we just want to hold on to it. But if you keep trying, it will happen and you will be curious if you can rid yourself of just a little more, and then just a little more still. Lakhiani's exercise confirmed for me that forgiveness was a trainable skill. And with this skill under my belt, I felt like I could run a forgiveness marathon!

THE BAD SIDE OF A 'GOOD SOLDIER'

While I had been diligently working on forgiveness and waiting for it to take hold as a strategy for thriving, I continued to scramble as a single mom, doing my best to keep everything just as it was when I had a husband to share in the everyday household and parenting responsibilities. I was learning the value of forgiveness, but in a compartmentalized way. Turns out, I had focused on the obstacles I could see, but there were obstacles I was missing that were really holding me back from fully accepting my current circumstances and getting to where I wanted to be. I call this discovery the "Good Soldier" part of my journey.

Have you ever had a conversation and the person you're talking with makes what he or she thinks is a casual observation about you that literally redefines how you see yourself? One such moment came after chronicling the big events in my life to a friend and explaining what I'd done to get through them. After listening, my friend told me, "You've been being a good soldier." At first I thought that was cool. I liked the image of a soldier marching forward through varying obstacles, bearing burdens for others, donning battle scars from taking one for the team. But as we continued speaking and I tried it on further, we agreed the observation wasn't necessarily a compliment.

A good soldier commits to serving others and is willing to deny her own needs. Good soldiers are often seen as admirable. We all know them and have been them at certain times in our lives. The problem is that when you continually play the role of the good soldier, you may end up depleting your emotional and physical resources, and by that point you're not much good to anyone.

While you're so busy focusing on the well-being of others, the world is carrying on. One day, if you decide to stop to come up for air or are forced to look in the mirror, you'll likely find yourself tired, maybe empty or lost, and perhaps you might even be resentful. You've been busy holding everyone else up, and while they're soaring, you realize it's likely you'll never leave the ground. You risk playing a supporting role in your own life, never taking the reins. And what you actually do is rob yourself and even the people around you of the person you were put on this earth to be. You give away your own potential to be great.

Being the good soldier had been a pattern for me. As a daughter, sister, and mom, my instinct to support others first was, of course, natural. But I'd taken it to an unnatural place. Helping others is great, supporting your loved ones when they're down is a fundamental part of life, and it's not always helpful to assert your own needs in times of crisis. Empathy is a noble

THE BAD SIDE OF A 'GOOD SOLDIER'

quality and being a good soldier can teach you volumes about others.

But for me, being a good soldier had meant ignoring myself. I'd muted my voice; I'd corked my feelings. I'd marched forward in the name of my family, keeping my chin up through it all. I thought I was doing it out of love but I've since realized there was much more coming into play.

> *Sometimes you don't realize the weight of a burden you've been carrying until you feel the weight of its release.*
>
> *-Unknown*

Acting for others' sakes (and a lot of times it was more worrying about someone than actually acting on their behalf) meant that I didn't have to look inside and reflect. I didn't have to think about how I would face my own fears or what I would do with my future. I'd allowed myself a false sense of progress merely because I was busy thinking about someone else's situation. And though it seemed I had allowed myself to become disempowered, I had actually given myself a lot of power in that role.

Rarely speaking up to tell my parents I missed them gave me the power to think I had personally contributed to them coming through the loss of Amy and to their being happy. Being completely exhausted, but staying up late with my son while he did his homework each night meant he needed me and that I had the power to prevent him from feeling abandoned or alone. It gave me the power to think that I was totally responsible for him feeling supported, even though he had his siblings, his friends, and his dad was just a phone call away. Driving my kids in every which direction for five hours each day in lieu of organizing carpools gave me the power to think I was the only one who could get them places safely and on time.

I couldn't control everything in their lives, but in the areas I could govern, I did everything humanly possible to make my kids feel normal in the months following the breakup of my marriage. I overthought their future. I thought of a thousand things that could negatively affect their development and did everything I could think of to counter them. They couldn't have healthy, loving relationships if their parents didn't interact with each other, right? So I arranged for their father to come to my home twice a week and cook them dinner. That way they could be in their normal environment with dad and we would briefly chat about daily happenings as I grabbed my purse and my keys on the way out the door. But that also meant that twice a week I had to leave my own environment for a few hours. I had to leave my own home.

"You're designing a life without any time and space dedicated to yourself," my friend told me. I sort of knew this beforehand, but I really didn't care because I was being a good soldier by doing the work I saw as necessary to hold everyone up around me. I'd created a scenario that gave me the power to think that everyone else's well-being depended on me, so much so that I was supposed to be a martyr for their happiness. Now that was a weird and unwelcome discovery.

I want to be clear in that I don't regret any of what I do on behalf of my family and in most instances I am right where I want to be, doing exactly what I want to be doing. I love parenting and the responsibilities that come with it. I love spending time in the car with my kids and sitting up with them while they work. And when I came up with the idea to have their dad come to my home to cook dinner, a counselor agreed that would be great for the kids.

The issue was that I was prepared to do this at any cost. And that, I'm pretty sure, was not healthy. There were only so many hours in the day, and the demands would always exceed my available time. At some point, something would have to give. And I was always prepared to make it me.

In essence, I had grown powerless as my own person. I'd spent years stagnant, standing in front of the same wall, day after day, so that others could stand on my shoulders and jump over it. I was doing not only myself but those around me a disservice by not climbing over it myself. I was being left behind.

I used to hate it when people would say to me "don't forget to take care of yourself." In a time of crisis and when people are depending on you, that seemed so selfish. And, by the way, what did that even look like? After the good soldier discovery, however, I realized that it's not selfish to look after yourself, and I was going to have to figure out what that meant. I wasn't going to get massages and pedicures. Well, maybe I could get used to that, but it would have to be more, too! I began to understand that as long as you're looking after the people that you care about when they need you, and that you feel content that you are doing your personal best in supporting them, it's not only okay but fundamental to consider your own well-being.

I now understood I had a responsibility to serve myself just as I did my kids. If I asked them to be the best they could be, why shouldn't I ask the same of myself? I'd watch them and encourage them to be independent, take care of their bodies, rest when they needed to, play when they should, risk failure, and dream wildly. I had ignored my responsibility to myself, however, and wasn't walking my talk. Although now I can honestly say I deserve my well-being without feeling the need to justify it to myself, at the time it felt counterintuitive.

I would have to go way off course in my thinking to embrace my own needs and wants. Dreaming about my own future after my family is grown or being gentle with myself when I am just too tired to wait up until curfew, would have to involve self-directed growth and I would need to tackle this as part of my system for thriving. The day I learned the bad side of being a good soldier was the day I started learning to be me again.

Before we say goodbye to these murky territories of grief and disappointing discoveries, I'd like to discuss one last grievance-related experience of mine: parenting through grief.

Now there are two sides to this balancing act. The first seems, especially immediately following the tragedy, very overwhelming. This is being depended on. It's stressful. I had three kids in their most impressionable years when their dad and I split up, and they were looking to me for answers. They needed me to be a rock at a time when I was reeling so hard I couldn't find the ground to plant my feet. How do you provide answers that you don't have? How do you set an example when you don't have one in front of you? I was constantly afraid I would steer them in the wrong direction. What if the divorce didn't seem to hit me hard enough? Well, that could alienate and really hurt them. What if it seemed to hit me too hard? Then they could live in constant worry that I wasn't going to be okay and that their home life would be unstable. These types of questions filled my head all day long and I had no idea how I might be affecting my children.

But after a certain point, I learned about the second side of this balancing act. This side I refer to as the privilege of being depended on. I realized at the end of the day, worrying about how my children might see me, striving to be a rock instead of a whirling dervish, was what gave me purpose. Parenting gave me an objective outside of myself. My sole responsibility was not just to *manage my own grief* but to *manage my grief properly*, for my children's sake. When you lose a loved one or a job or a marriage, the fact that you are a parent can actually pose a powerful and very motivating question: How in these challenging circumstances do I continue to make my life worthy of my children?

FORGIVING YOURSELF

So there I was, a Weeble, a forgiveness-marathoner, and a rock for my kids. But I had also now discovered the bad part of the good soldier in me, and it didn't feel too good.

I felt like I had been hiding out from the world as I was intended to experience it in being unhealthily preoccupied with everyone else's well-being and in forgiving everything around me. I felt like I had not been engaging with the world authentically, and as Molly Biehl, I had been playing small. I kept putting off things I wanted to do, convincing myself I'd have the opportunity another day. I'd lost a sister at twenty-six and a dad at fifty-nine and my hunch is they'd have something to say about life's guarantees.

Then one night when I had stayed home instead of attending a party I'd been invited to, I began to examine why I had declined to attend. This particular night, the typical excuses didn't seem to be holding up. I wasn't especially tired. I had nowhere to be in the morning. I liked everyone who was going to be there, and there would even be music and dancing. And it hit me like a ton of bricks — I was ashamed. I had been hiding out from the world that particular evening because I was ashamed to be alone. And, as I began to sit with that, I realized that I was ashamed of a great deal more.

I was ashamed I would never be the daughter my parents had in my late sister in terms of accomplishments or the "cool factor." I was ashamed I could not be a good enough wife to make my ex-husband want to stick around. I was ashamed that I had stayed out of the workforce and now found myself jobless with few relevant skills, and I was ashamed that I had felt destined for tragedy.

> *Have patience with all things. But first of all, with yourself.*
>
> *– St. Francis De Sales*

It felt insane to have just now been coming to

this realization. All this time trying to be a rock for others — trying to forgive other people, to forgive the world around me — it hadn't occurred to me at all to give myself any slack. I had put so much pressure on myself to do right by everyone else but not to do right by me, and I risked my self-esteem.

In that moment I deeply felt that in trying so hard for all those years, that in masking my grief by doing for others, I had unequivocally earned the right to forgive myself for any wrongdoing. Finally, I was on the brink of triumph.

You better believe it when I tell you that my journey through grief ended with that corny forgiveness exercise. This time I didn't have to imagine the person I was forgiving. I just had to look in the mirror.

FORGIVING YOURSELF

It was ultimately releasing my shame and forgiving myself that was the most freeing experience of them all. Where my head had been full of fear and self-admonishments, it now has peace and self-acceptance. And when you are in that space - through that shift in thinking - there is room to hope and dream. To understand what I've been through and be excited for where I'm going was a journey truly worth taking. I've shared it now. I've found my voice. Maybe one of you will be willing to do the same.

EPILOGUE

I recently had a conversation with my sister Kim. It was Christmas and we'd just finished talking about the gifts we'd planned for our nieces and nephews when I asked her, "Hey! Did you know I'm writing a book?"

"Yeah mom mentioned something about it,"

she said. "Are you actually getting that off the ground?"

"Yep. I'm writing away as we speak."

Her response was a familiar one: "You seriously started writing a book in the middle of the holidays?! Why doesn't that surprise me?"

"You know I've always wanted to write one, and I guess the impulse was strong enough this time." I thought about it for a moment. "My plan was always 2019. That's what I had written down and pictured happening for months now, but it became a little funny thinking that I should wait another two years to get something out of me that has been building for twenty-three. So I'm going for it now."

"Well, what's it about?"

EPILOGUE

I told her: It's about my journey through my series of challenges, about being intentional and forgiving in tough situations. It's about triumph after grief.

"That's awesome!" She said. "I wish I had a copy of it now. I'm meeting up with someone tomorrow who could use some hope."

This piqued my interest. "Who is it?"

"Someone I know whose son died recently. I can tell that she doesn't feel like she'll ever be motivated to do much of anything again. It's a familiar feeling; I remember writing in my

> *Grief is like an ocean; it comes in waves, ebbing and flowing. Sometimes the water is calm and sometimes it is overwhelming. All we can do is learn to swim.*
>
> *– Vicki Harrison*

journal just after Amy died that I didn't believe I'd ever smile again." I imagined her smiling ear-to-ear. "I want her to know that she will."

"Yes!" I responded. "I had a similar experience, when I felt a spring in my step. It was the first time since Amy passed and I'd come to think it would never return. I was so excited that I raced over to my cubicle mate to share with him the great news! I remember him looking at me and smiling like, 'Way to go, you've got this!'"

"Right?" she said "It's great when you get to tell someone who's feeling stuck and alone that it gets better."

Indeed, we all have our stories. Although circumstances are different and we process things uniquely, we can benefit so much when we share. The obstacles one person faces might seem from ground-level to be taller than another person's, but the fact is we all get stuck for a while. It's just a matter of listening to yourself and learning from others, and you will get moving again. While our conversation was about a solemn thing, my sister and I could still celebrate being in the "You've Got This!" club. And, we could celebrate, hopeful that her friend, and countless others, could be in our club eventually, too.

ABOUT THE AUTHOR

OVERVIEW

In 2017 Molly Biehl will officially launch her new business, "A Triumphant Me" along with her first book, "You've Got This!" She is on a mission to empower women to overcome hardships and achieve their wildest dreams. A resilient woman herself, Molly is devoted to sharing her strategies to overcome grief and stand tall in the midst of challenges.

While speaking to audiences around the world, her goal is to impact the lives of 26,000 women who need encouragement to bounce back and live their best lives.

WHO IS MOLLY BIEHL?

Molly Biehl is a mother, speaker and coach, dedicated to empowering women to bounce back from life's setbacks and achieve their wildest dreams. At the age of 23, Molly faced one of her greatest challenges; the untimely death of her sister who was brutally murdered in South Africa while serving as a Fulbright scholar and an anti-apartheid activist.

In the years following the tragedy, Molly discovered an important truth- grief doesn't have to define who you are, instead it can refine your identity so that you can become someone whose life is a source of inspiration and not despair.

She recounts her story of resilience in the book, *"You've Got This!"* Molly hopes her writing will serve as hope to women everywhere who are longing to tap into their own inner strength and become the best version of themselves, just as she has.

ABOUT THE BOOK

Like a phoenix rising out of the ashes, so too will women who are experiencing grief overcome, after reading *You've Got This!* The book journeys through different stages of dealing with tragedy and offers strategies to triumph in the midst of it all.

Author Molly Biehl, chronicles her journey of divorce, dealing with death, and ultimately forgiving her sister's killers.

You've Got This! is ideal for anyone who is facing difficulties and may not know what to do next. Molly reminds readers that there is light at the end of the tunnel and it gets brighter the more purposeful you become.

SPEAKING TOPICS & WORKSHOPS

Life Begins Outside of Your Comfort Zone

Some people live with regrets, while others live with exciting stories how they dared to push life to its limits and take risks. The story that you will tell depends on how willing you are to step out of your comfort zone and into the realm of possibility. Learn how to become a risk-taker, a leader, and live out your passion while changing the world.

The Power of Forgiveness

The quote by Dr. King, "forgiveness is not an occasional act, it is a constant attitude," captures exactly what it took for Molly Biehl to forgive the breakdown of her marriage, her sister's killers and even herself. Forgiveness has to become part of your character in order for it to work its magic. As a speaker Molly shares her strategies to break free from the prison of anger and reclaim your excitement for life.

Previous Engagements

BIOGRAPHY

A former marathoner and mother to 3 teenagers, Molly Biehl likes journeying through life in the fast lane.

The third of 4 children, Molly spent her formative years in Santa Fe, NM then Newport Beach, CA. She was exposed to great ethnic and socioeconomic diversity and, experiencing the sharp contrasts between poor and affluent communities, understood early on the value of resilience and the importance of serving others.

Throughout her life, Molly has served as a volunteer. While in graduate school she worked with inner-city youth and families in New Orleans. Her passion for working with the underserved took on new heights when she traveled to South Africa to pioneer a reading program through the Amy Biehl Foundation Trust, an organization created to honor the legacy of her late sister. She dedicates herself to being a life-long learner and to helping others discover their untapped potential.

Through her work in literacy and public schools, Molly is passionate about sharing her love for education and service with the next generation.

Despite the challenges of several family tragedies, Molly is a consummate example of a triumphant woman. In the next phase of her life, she hopes to inspire women to stand tall in the face of adversity and live their best lives.

Contact: Molly Biehl
Gmail: ATriumphantMe@gmail.com
Website: www.ATriumphantMe.com

This book is a production of
A Triumphant Me, LLC and published
by Laptop Lifestyle, LLC.

For more information
call 1-868-374-7441 or
visit LaptopLifestyle.org

Your story is waiting to be told!

A TRIUMPHANT ME

LAPTOP
Lifestyle

Made in the USA
San Bernardino, CA
11 February 2017